MUSHROOMS

Lm 8/82.

Examines the health-giving properties of mushrooms and gives advice on how to cultivate them and how to use them in preparing appetizing and health-giving meals.

MUSHROOMS

Nature's Major Protein Food

by
G.J. BINDING, M.B.E., F.R.H.S.

NATURE'S WAY

THORSONS PUBLISHERS LIMITED
Wellingborough, Northamptonshire

First published as
About Mushrooms in 1972
First published in the *Nature's Way* series 1978

ISBN 0 7225 0195 1

*Made and Printed in Great Britain by
Weatherby Woolnough, Wellingborough
Northants, England, NN8 4BX*

CONTENTS

ACKNOWLEDGEMENTS

I wish to express my sincere thanks for all the help given in the preparation of this book by:

W.R. Alderton, Esquire,
    Secretary, Mushroom Growers' Association,
    Agriculture House, Knightsbridge,
    London S.W.1

Ronald B. Hunte, Esquire,
    Executive Director,
    American Mushroom Institute,
    Kennett Square,
    Pennsylvania, U.S.A.

F.W. Toovey, Esquire, O.B.E., B.Sc., A.R.C.S., A.I.C.T.A.
    Director, Glasshouse Crops, Research Centre,
    Rustington, Littlehampton, Sussex.

Martha Baker,
    Publisher, *Brandywine Bugle*,
    Westown, Philadelphia, U.S.A.

Mushroom & Horticulture (BMI) Products,
    421-425 London Road,
    Mitcham, Surrey.

INTRODUCTION

DURING THE PAST twenty-five years a revolution has taken place in the art of mushroom growing; the cultivation of the crop is no longer so much a gamble or game of chance against the elements, pests and diseases. With the tremendous boom in the production of crops the price of mushrooms to buyers and housewives has been reduced to a quarter of what it was twenty years ago. Few commodities, especially foodstuffs, are ever likely to have their price reduced; mushrooms, however, are cheaper now than ever before. As a result the mushroom is no longer a luxury food for those who can afford it but is marketed at prices within the reach of all. Likewise, mushroom farming today will not make one rich after a few years.

Commercial mushroom cultivation in England has become quite a big business. During the years 1946/47 farmers only produced some 2,000,000 lbs of mushrooms but in less than twenty-five years the crop has expanded to 90,000,000 lbs and this year's harvest is expected to exceed 100,000,000 lbs with an estimated annual growth at the rate of some ten per cent. Today fifteen mushroom farms in England cultivate some sixty-five per cent of the entire crop. Twenty-five years ago growers could expect to receive 40p per lb for mushrooms gathered: today the price paid is less than 15p per lb. Mushroom farmers are now able to cultivate massive crops providing a ready market is available, but unlike most crops, storage life is very limited. The mushroom crop also serves a useful purpose in supplying the canning industry with button mushrooms, mushroom soups, and dried mushrooms. An increasing percentage of crops is being used by frozen food companies, especially in America. The figures of crops being cultivated does not take into consideration the large quantity grown by amateurs and part-time gardeners, many of whom have become experts at their often profitable hobby. Most companies specializing in supplying mushroom growing kits are prepared to purchase growers' crops.

For a long time it was considered that mushrooms, like certain other foods, were simply delicacies with no particular health-giving properties. We now know that this vegetable contains a good supply of protein, vitamins, minerals and other essentials; this knowledge has played a part in increasing demand for the crop.

Ancient herbalists were for centuries aware of the curative powers of the mushroom and the fact that many edible species of fungi could be found in the English countryside. All mushrooms are fungi but not all fungi are mushrooms, which comprise the fleshy parts of certain fungi.

Generally speaking few people dislike mushrooms but occasionally one meets a person who is allergic to them. During the war years the crop suffered a set-back owing to the shortage of manures, for farmers were not encouraged to grow a vegetable demanding massive amounts of compost. All this has been changed, for in agricultural circles today the mushroom rates high as a food crop.

In this little introduction to the mushroom a brief outline of its history is given in France, Italy, England and America. We also examine the protein, vitamin, mineral and other health-giving ingredients of this vegetable. The peculiar healing powers of fungi from the days of folklore are also explored. For those gardening enthusiasts who are prepared to explore the possibilities of growing mushrooms brief cultural instructions about crops are discussed. The closing chapter provides recipes from many countries showing some of the endless ways of producing appetizing and health-giving meals of mushrooms for every occasion from breakfast to supper.

CHAPTER ONE

HISTORY OF THE MUSHROOM

THE MUSHROOM IS a very ancient vegetable which has been prized as a delicacy for hundreds of years but it is only since the end of the seventeenth century that growers began to gradually master the art of cultivating crops under controlled conditions. Before this time mushrooms were simply gathered from the farmland, fields and meadows frequented by cattle and horses, where masses of this delicious little vegetable would spring up every autumn, and to a lesser degree during the month of June. Even after crops could be grown under cover it took a long time before the uncertainty was almost completely eliminated. Long years of experiments with trial and error methods had to be carried out before the large ever-expanding crops of recent years could be cultivated successfully. What is also most important is that growers today can supply the market in an expert way to meet public demands. Much progress has been made since those days when the only way of getting mushrooms was to seek them in the autumn when they grew wild. Crops are now available fresh, tinned, dried and — more recently — frozen.

Ancient History
As long ago as 300 B.C. Theophrastus recorded that

mushrooms were valued as a food and for export. During the centuries which followed well-known Romans including Cicero, Juvenal and Pliny all considered the mushroom to be a great but expensive delicacy. The crop, growing in a wild state, continued to be accepted and provided tasty dishes throughout the Middle Ages. In Italy and France the mushroom was also popular, though all these years ago people had little or no knowledge of the true food value of this fungus. It was in the latter country during the reign of Louis XIV that mushrooms were gradually brought under crude control, as a crop, by being cultivated in caves near Paris.

The exact time when mushrooms were used as a food is not very clear. History or fable tells that Claudius, the stepfather of Nero, the Emperor, died of poisoning after consuming fungus served in mistake for mushrooms. Wild mushrooms, in common with other fungus, are known to have grown in Europe for over 2,000 years but an element of doubt always existed when some species proved to be poisonous. The work of the early French growers led to our present-day safe crops. They were the first to master the art of controlled mushroom culture, thus paving the way for intensive cultivation and final acceptance by people of a fine food crop perfectly safe to eat. In spite of this it was not until many years later that the mushroom became available on English markets. One of the reasons was that for a long time the French kept their methods of artificial cultivation a closely guarded secret.

Folklore
The mushroom has always been surrounded by superstitions and in some places still is to a certain extent. An ancient belief which still lingers suggests

that mushrooms were in some way connected with the supernatural and would grow overnight, as masses appeared suddenly, as if by magic. This is of course only because ninety per cent of the growth takes place beneath the surface; in ancient times people were unaware of this and thought a crop had appeared in a few hours. In all, about eight weeks is required for this vegetable to mature.

Old stories also connected mushrooms with fairies and when they grew in circles these were said to be fairy rings. There is of course a natural explanation accounting for the tendency of wild species to appear in the form of a circle. In folklore, too, mushrooms are credited with having some mysterious power to aid cancer sufferers. (Mushrooms and cancer are discussed in Chapter Two.)

Sayings and superstitions of long ago die hard and it is rather unfortunate that even today some people do not accept the mushroom as being of excellent food value. A large number of species of wild fungi can be consumed but there are twelve which can cause poisoning.

Medical Herbalists

Practically every growing plant including flowers, vegetables and even weeds were used in one form or another in ancient times by practitioners of herbal medicine. Therefore, it is not surprising that mushrooms played a part, herbalists being mainly concerned with two species, the *Puffball* and *Fly Agaric*. Pieces of dried inner substance from puffballs, when ripe, contain a mass of spores resembling powder. This 'powder' was said to be especially good for treating the sore legs of horses. Puffballs were used as surgical applications for deep cuts or treating ounds and abrasions. This mushroom also proved very good for stopping bleeding and healing sores, a fine ripe species being used for this purpose. A medical tincture was obtained by rubbing this mushroom and its spores with invert sugar; this being used for the purpose of treating headaches.

France

The early French method of cultivating mushrooms was described by an author in a book published in Paris in 1707. Briefly, the system consisted of preparing horse manure and planting spores from wild mushrooms into it. About a hundred years later mushroom cultivation was taking place in underground quarries near Paris. After horse manure became composted it was laid out in ridges and injected with mushroom spawn taken from supplies growing wild in fields and meadows. Results could be obtained from this simple method but an element of doubt always existed and on many occasions a crop just did not appear. In 1808 a French grower named Renaudot planted crops in twenty miles of caves and harvested an average of 3,000 lbs of mushrooms daily. So the French during their early days of cultivation treated mushroom spores as seeds. Beds were prepared under cover, using a two-inch layer of composted horse manure. A ripe mushroom, one of the finest species of a crop, was selected. This specimen, loaded with spores, was then put head first into the compost which was made firm all round. If such plantings were successful, a number of spores would germinate, resulting in sufficient spawn being obtained to grow crops. This method is of course no longer used but was for a long time widely accepted in many countries even up to the Second World War, the spawn being taken and put into fields and meadows. The problems were that the spawn thus planted was exposed to fluctuating weather conditions, diseases, and attacks from all manner of insects. So there was little or no guarantee of a worthwhile crop. In spite of all setbacks and complications it is interesting to know that mushroom spawn has been known to remain alive for extremely long periods, over one hundred years in fact. This sometimes results in mushrooms appearing as if by magic on lawns laid in towns far away from fields and meadows where the spawn impregnated the turf. The name mushroom comes from the French word *mousseron*, in spite of the fact that in France they are called *champigons*. The Germans, French, Italians and other Continental people have a far greater knowledge of species of mushrooms growing wild than most people in England. In spite of this some 300 persons die each year in France from eating poisonous toadstools. We are more fortunate in England for it is some time since anyone died from eating a poisonous plant or fungus.

Early mushroom growers in England took a great interest in the French methods and were fortunate in having an abundance of wild mushroom spawn in fields and meadows. The industry made rapid progress and by about 1800 English 'brick' spawn was being exported to many countries, including America and even Australia. In spite of this, however, the entire system left much to be desired. The 'brick' spawn — composed of horse and cow manures — frequently harboured all manner of insect pests, weed seeds, and other moulds, and would not always produce a good strain of mushrooms. The fact that this very dubious spawn was so widely accepted shows just what a problem the entire business of growing a mushroom crop presented.

Our large mushroom crop today is no longer just

an autumn one as is the case under natural growing conditions, but can be cultivated all the year round. Mushroom cultivation in England rates high among our agricultural produce and crops are administered and growers given help by the Mushroom Growers' Association, a specialist branch of The National Farmers' Union. United Kingdom mushroom production was 90,000,000 lbs in 1970 with a value to the growers of about £13-14,000,000. Future crops are likely to exceed 100,000,000 lbs annually. Hotels, shops and catering establishments with an ever-increasing demand for more mushrooms make commercial growing worthwhile. It is forecast that the crop will expand at the rate of about ten per cent annually. This present stage of perfection has taken a long time to be reached for England lagged behind France in spite of appeals from growers and authors that increased cultivation would prove a great asset.

Many Species

Prior to the appearance of our bumper crops of cultivated mushrooms which have been produced in England since the last war, nature somewhat compensated our forefathers by providing over a hundred edible species which grew wild in the countryside. The St. George mushroom was one of the first to become popular in our kitchens.

The puffball was also one of the finest species of mushrooms found in our countryside during the heyday of herbal medicine. In Norfolk large puffballs appeared on margins of cornfields and these were sometimes called 'Bulfers' or 'Bulfists'. They would also abound in the autumn, popping up as if by magic on lawns, heaths and pastures, often appearing in corners of orchards and even in gardens, in fact, puffballs were everywhere. These beautiful species would range in size from that of a turnip to gigantic ones as big as a man's head. Puffballs are oval in shape and depressed on top, with a smooth surface which cracks as the fungus ripens. The flesh of this species should be pure white right through and this is a sure sign that they are edible.

Long ago in England and Italy young pulpy puffballs were served as delicious feasts. On preparation the very large ones were often cut into slices ¼ inch thick, dipped in egg yolk and cooked in fresh butter with herbs. They were also served as tasty omelettes. Long ago it was realized that mushrooms contained phosphate of potassium, and, as we now know from modern research, they are rich in many other essentials.

In 1883 The Society of Amateur Botanists came into being whilst members sat down to a meal of puffballs served with tea.

Fly Agaric

This species consists of a large convex shaped mushroom of a deep orange/scarlet colour with white gills. The name came into being because of its use with milk to destroy flies. A similar fungus was the bug agaric or flybane, so named because it proved very effective for destroying bugs after being spread on beds. This species is dangerous and its red upper surface is covered with warts. If consumed in error it will cause such effects as intoxication, delirium, and even death, owing to its potent narcotic strength. Appearing in dry locations such as pine and birch woods, the fly agaric is more frequent in Scotland than England. Being so powerful it was used with caution by the herbalists of old and no doubt caused many people in those days to view all mushrooms with suspicion. Even today delicious cultivated mushrooms which are one hundred per cent safe should be cooked and consumed without undue delay after being gathered. Raw in salads, for instance, they are quite delicious. They should never be cooked, put in a refrigerator and later reheated. It is also not advisable to take strong alcohol such as spirits with a meal in which mushrooms are included.

Fumes from burning fungus were at one time used by doctors as a chloroform to assist in performing minor speedy operations prior to more efficient methods being found.

When fungus was burnt the fumes were sufficiently narcotic to overcome a swarm of bees, thus allowing beekeepers to remove their honey; the swarm recovered later with no ill effects after their deep sleep. Today we have aids such as protective clothing for beekeepers to wear as a safeguard against stings.

Sterilized Mushroom Spawn

In 1893 the French brought a drastic change to the cultivation of mushrooms when, at the Pasteur Institute in Paris, they were able to produce 'sterilized' or 'pure culture' mushroom spawn for the first time. France was thus able to dominate the world in the cultivated mushroom crop. Commercial business being highly competitive the French kept the manner in which they developed mushroom spawn a closely guarded secret. In 1900 the Americans likewise devised a method of sterilizing spawn but it was still another thirty years before it was produced in England. The advent of cultured spawn took much of the uncertainty out of mushroom growing and as a result fine crops were soon being cultivated in many countries. Furthermore, growers were for the first time able to make a more accurate forecast of annual plantings in order to try and make supply meet demands.

Old-Time Tests.

A method proved to have been reliable long ago for checking if wild mushrooms were safe to eat was to cook them together with a small peeled onion. If after boiling for a few minutes the onion remained white and clean, it was a sure sign the mushrooms were edible. If the onion turned blue or black, poisonous species were present, a sign that the entire contents should be discarded. An ancient practice of testing wild species for safety with a silver spoon is not considered effective, in spite of the fact that they do contain sulphur. A cure for poison caused by consuming inedible mushrooms was given by Celsus, who said: 'If anyone shall have eaten noxious fungi let him take radishes with vinegar and water or with salt and water.' An ancient guide as to when wild mushrooms were safe for would-be hunters was given in these words, 'When the moon is at the full, mushrooms you may freely pull. But when the moon is on the wane wait till you think to pluck again.' No wonder people so long ago considered this tasty vegetable to be closely connected with the supernatural.

Advice to Old-Time Growers

About 1860 a pamphlet on mushroom growing appeared which was believed to have been published by Baron Vander Linden d'Hoegverst. The translation of these instructions gives an interesting account of the cultivation of mushrooms over a hundred years ago. It reads:

> The cultivation of the mushroom so often described has seldom been accomplished successfully by those who have undertaken it. Chance alone has made it succeed in certain cases; and I am one of those who have found, that, for two or three years a crop was secured which the following

year failed, although the measures used were in all respects the same as those first adopted. After observations extended over a series of years I think I can safely attribute this difficulty to three causes — to damp, drought or bad spawn. It was remarked long ago when little rain falls in May or June but few mushrooms are found in the fields in the following September, because the spawn which forms during that season and of which a portion remains over from the previous year cannot be developed and is thus wasted. Keeping these observations in view I only water my beds four weeks after they are made and then only when I see at the surface the tips of the mushrooms or small threads that indicate the presence of spawn. To prevent the soil which should be damp from forming too hard a crust I cover the beds with hay or aftermath thrown on lightly. I have also used with success for this purpose old carpets, always however, putting a little aftermath beneath them. This serves two purposes, stops beds from becoming dry, and prevents propagation of insects. Good spawn vital.

During 1880 mushrooms were said to be one of the most delicate but appreciated vegetables cultivated. The French, from their earliest crops, sent supplies to London markets. Even in these early days of mushroom growing, if good spawn was obtained and introduced at the right time, reasonable results could be expected.

The Mushroom Growers' Association

The British Mushroom Growers' Association was not formed till after the Second World War and by this time public opinion had long been misled into regarding the crop as simply a luxury food. A priority task of the newly formed Association was to influence the Government by proving mushrooms to be a valuable food crop. This was carried out and the Ministry of Agriculture finally accepted mushrooms as a nutritious food with much to offer the population. The tremendous goodness in crops was confirmed by research in America, one of the first countries to recognize the true value of the mushroom as a vital food.

As Old as History

Mushrooms, in all shapes, sizes and colours have existed since the countryside appeared. As with all fungi, mushrooms were always viewed with suspicion in the Middle Ages. Toadstools and mushrooms were thought to be used in the night by creatures intent on bringing harm to humans.

Gradually people began to experiment with the mushroom as a food; it was established that most varieties are edible and we now know they have been consumed for centuries. The Chaldeans of the Bible and the ancient Chinese, Japanese and Indians all ate mushrooms obtained fresh from the fields. They also preserved or dried them in powder form for a tasty addition to meals. The Romans regarded mushrooms as something extra special and slaves, employed to collect them, were flogged if they failed to hand in all that were gathered. Special cooking pots were also introduced by the Romans and used entirely for preparing mushrooms.

The Americans were the first to obtain spores of a fine mushroom, *Agararicus Campestris*, and from this produce excellent cultivated mushrooms perfectly safe to eat. Even today, gathering wild mushrooms requires considerable experience, for there is no real test to ensure that those growing wild are edible.

CHAPTER TWO

MUSHROOMS IN AMERICA

FIRST RECORDS OF the introduction of controlled mushroom growing in the U.S.A. show this to have taken place in 1880 in the vicinity of New York and on Long Island. Like their French pioneers these early American growers produced crops in caves and cellars. It was another five years before nurserymen started to experiment with the growing of mushrooms beneath benches in greenhouses in Kennett Square, Pennsylvania. These growers cultivated tasty mushrooms as a sideline to their masses of blooms, little realizing that they were sowing the seeds of what has subsequently proved to be the largest, highest concentrated and most profitable mushroom growing business in the U.S.A., if not the entire world. Being experts in the art of the cultivation of every kind of flower, these pioneers possessed that commonly found asset of 'green fingers' and so quickly mastered the skills of mushroom cultivation. Within one year the first of the special purpose-built mushroom houses were being constructed in the Kennett Square area. By 1896 it was apparent that the mushroom crops of Kennett Square had a rosy future. Last year, 1971, was the seventy-fifth anniversary of the building of the first mushroom growing houses in America

Rapid Growth
Later the cultivation of the mushroom spread to New York State, the Mid West and the Pacific Coast. However, the heart and soul and most intensive cultivation of this fine crop remained in Kennett

Square, Pennsylvania, where the American Mushroom Institute was formed. Of the 800 growers in the United States today, 600 of them have flourishing businesses in Pennsylvania. Figures issued by the United States Department of Agriculture show that the total mushroom production in Pennsylvania, Maryland and Delaware for 1965-66 equalled over 95,000,000 lbs valued at more than $29,000,000 and of this massive crop Kennett Square produced eighty-five per cent. The forecast for July 1971, according to the American Mushroom Institute, is that the crop will exceed the 200,000,000 lb mark. From these early beginnings an enterprising industry has been built up. For decades this fungus had been considered an expensive luxury beyond the means of many and giving no great food value. It is now readily available at a reasonable price and highly valued as a food. The mushroom in America has come into its own as a main crop in the Chester County of Pennsylvania. In this area the extent of its growth has resulted in mushrooms becoming of greater economic importance as a food crop than either fruit or vegetables. There is no truer saying than that the American crop has 'mushroomed' in every sense of the word, making this fine appetizing vegetable available to everyone at prices comparing more than favourably with other foods.

The Americans have certainly made great strides in the art of cultivating mushrooms and have probably done more than most to probe the centuries-old secrets of this little fungus. Nutrition is really only in its infancy regarding vitamins, minerals and all the other goodness provided from health-giving crops of all kinds. Much more has to be learnt for it was only about fifty years ago that the first vitamin was discovered and although considerable progress has

been made, many questions still remain unanswered.
It is a far more complex problem than is at first
realized, for, in many areas of the world with extreme
variations of climate there are no hard and fast rules
appertaining to the entire population. Generally,
people thrive and remain healthy by consuming
crops, vegetables, and fruit indigenous to the land in
which they live. For long years the risks of eating
fungi were great and people became poisoned. This
danger still exists, even today, if wild mushrooms are
gathered by persons unable to identify species of
fungi which are safe to eat. With such risks constantly
present it is sometimes wondered why primitive man
took the hazardous chance of eating wild mushrooms.
In many cases it may well have been simply a case of
finding food to survive but credit must be given to
the mushroom for being a very tasty and most
satisfying vegetable. As progress has been made in
civilization man has gradually rated eating in terms of
pleasure derived from food, this often resulting in a
constant search for new, ever increasing exotic
supplies for the table. Mushrooms for a long time
came into this category, being both expensive and
considered a delicacy. The American extensive
culture of the mushroom with detailed investigation
into its nutritive value helped to pave the way for
crops in many parts of the world.

Health-Giving Foods

In spite of all the adulteration, artificial colouring and
preservatives that go into our food today many
people are very much interested in obtaining good
whole foods in their most natural state. American
scientists and nutrition experts have presented the
world with some fine worthwhile foods. For long
years spinach was simply ignored until after the First

World War when in America folic acid was first isolated in this vegetable. Thus an aid for the prevention or cure of pernicious anaemia was suddenly found in a vegetable crop of which there are numerous species, all easy to cultivate the year round. Spinach cultivation quickly became widespread in the United States and it was served with all manner of meals and massive crops were cultivated for canning and eventually freezing. Such colourful characters as 'Popeye the Sailorman' came into being to sell the idea of tinned spinach to the American people. Whether or not Popeye's muscles would be packed with dynamite after his feed of spinach remains doubtful but it was proved that the iron, folic acid, and other ingredients made it a fine food for everyone.

Celery is another fine crop which was extensively grown in America when its health-giving properties were revealed. It was found to contain minerals, vitamins, and is especially rich in sulphur, vital for the prevention or even cure of rheumatism. So it is with the mushroom crop, which has become widely accepted as a health-giving food.

Since the end of the Second World War the cultured mushroom has been grown in increasingly larger crops year after year. They are recognized as adding a wonderful flavour to soups, sauces, gravies and used as a garnish or accompanying dish with every main meal. Not only is it one of the richest sources of protein but contains many vitamins and minerals, most of which we need only in the smallest quantity to remain in good health. Some people were under the impression that the cultured mushroom is not of such good food value as the wild species; this theory has been entirely disproved. Cultivated crops are not only equally good nutritionally but are cleaner and free from diseases. So the humble little mushroom can play an important part in our diet today. For many years it was ignored by nutrition experts and many others who classed the mushroom with spices and condiments. This belief was strengthened in books on diet, nutrition and cookery. We now know that such experts and authors were sadly misinformed for in diets today the mushroom rates high on the list of health-giving foods but for many years it was completely ignored by food analysts.

Future Prospects

The progressive mushroom growing headquarters of America in South Chester City, Pennsylvania, can claim to have the most highly concentrated cultivation of this crop, certainly in the U.S.A., if not the entire world. Far and wide the mushroom is no longer accepted merely as a delicacy but as an important vegetable which has become as vital economically as any other fruit or vegetable crop. In spite of this, much misunderstanding still exists about the manner in which mushrooms are grown. However, one must not accept the simple explanation of how easy it is to become either an amateur or full-time grower. Mushroom growing is not an easy way to make a fortune though people assume it is so because of the enormous crops and rapid expansion. Nothing really could be farther from the truth or more misleading. Few crops require such exacting conditions and precise adherence to instructions and nursing as the mushroom, so no wonder the final dish presents such a tasty meal. At all times the grower must ensure that temperatures and humidity are ideal and be always on guard against insect pests and diseases.

The American growers selected the *Agaricus Bisphorus* as the cultured mushroom of their now enormous annual crop of today.

With all the disasters and setbacks that may befall the prospective grower in America, or elsewhere, most persons with sufficient interest who are prepared to be devoted to the task and work hard can still do well in mushroom growing today. Those without capital will only succeed by hard work and constantly learning more about the art. Better than ever means of culture has resulted in an increased yield per square foot from 1 lb in 1940 to some 2.4 lbs today — an almost 250 per cent crop increase in thirty years which perhaps constitutes a record in the farming of any vegetable crop in the world. Likewise the total American cultivation has tripled in the last twenty years. What is also most heartening to growers is the ever increasing demand for this tasty vegetable. In other countries, as in the U.S.A., the appreciation and fondness for this fine food has increased. The mushroom has been aptly named the small vegetable with the great flavour.

Variety
The pure white mushroom comprises the bulk of the American crop. These mushrooms, after being transported to market or kept in a refrigerator, are apt to turn a brownish colour. This has no effect on the nutritional value. There are two other types mainly cultivated in America, The French Cream (beige or off white) and The Hawaiian Brown or Brown Mushroom.

Research
There have been a number of American Mushroom Industry Research studies into crops. The findings clearly show that mushrooms are a very rich source of protein, phosphorus, iron, thiamine, riboflavin, niacin and other minerals. These tests were conducted by

comparison with twelve other vegetables and fruits. The only one of these slightly superior to the mushroom for goodness and vitamin content was the green pea. Mushrooms had the highest amount of riboflavin, niacin, phosphorus and fat (a vegetable fat which can easily be assimilated by the body). They were second in protein and all other minerals, third in iron and fourth in thiamine. Ideal for the figure conscious or persons definitely overweight, mushrooms are very low in calories. These studies showed a calorie fluctuation of from sixty-six to ninety calories to the lb. The sodium content was likewise low, making them ideal in the diet of persons with heart conditions, kidney complaints, hypertension and nephritis.

Advantages

Mushrooms are inexpensive, easy to prepare and there is no wastage at all. If the grower is unable to sell his crop in a fresh state the residue can be marketed for making soups, canning, dehydration and more recently sold to the frozen food companies. So the little mushroom has tremendous possibilities as a food for every occasion. It is of interest to note that in the U.S.A. as much as seventy per cent of the total crop is used by the canning industry for such foods as soups. This little fungus, increasing at the rate of about 4,000,000 lbs annually, has brought changes to the American diet.

In these days of ever increasing food prices the cost of the humble little mushroom has gone down faster over the years than inflationary prices of meats, especially steak, have risen. So now is the time to reap the benefits of delicious tasty mushrooms, in many ways as good a food as steak and often less than half the price.

King Size

Some American cultured species of mushrooms are more than four inches in diameter and weigh over three ounces each. Mushrooms may be served at any meal from breakfast to supper. With no waste, and being easy to prepare and cook, the mushroom is a boon to the housewife, café owner, hotel proprietor or even the bachelor. Without doubt this little fungus is one of the most versatile and nutritious foods available today.

Mushrooms and Cancer

Certain claims have been made that mushrooms may act as a cancer deterrent. How true is this statement?

As we have seen, the French were the first to discover the secret of obtaining mushroom spawn, which in turn led to the cultivated mushroom. They kept their methods secret. It is an interesting fact that French growers, one and all, have for one hundred years been safeguarded against the dreaded disease of cancer. Can it be that the mineral salts of this unusual crop give protection if made part of the diet over a long period? Can a regular diet of mushrooms act as a prevention against this baffling illness? The human body has an inbuilt resistance to disease if we allow this to be developed by means of a correct diet. For centuries herbs, flowers and vegetables were used not only in the treatment of sickness and diseases, but also in a preventative manner. Scientists are now able to prove that many natural foods contain vitamins, minerals and other health-giving properties.

Nobel Prize Winner

Mr. Graham Chedd, Assistant Editor, writing in *The New Scientist* on the 11th May 1967, records that 'retine', which appears in body cells, can retard growth of tumours. He also stated that this compound can be produced and may result in a natural, safe and effective anti-cancer drug. This interesting discovery was made by Nobel Prize winner Albert Szent-Gyorgyi at The Institute of Muscle Research, Marine Biological Laboratory, Woods Hale, Massachusetts, U.S.A. Szent-Gyorgyi discovered what he termed 'promine', a substance which promotes the growth of cells in multicellular organisms; and 'retine' which retards such growth. It seems the human body has to strike a balance between 'promine' and 'retine' and in the normal course of events 'retine' predominates except in the case of those unfortunate persons who develop cancerous cells. This modern research and ancient beliefs of folklore coincide when it is shown that the edible mushroom the *Agaricus Campestris* or *Bisphorus* does in fact contain a rich supply of 'retine'.

The amount of 'retine' found in such mushrooms is as high as three units per millimetre of pressed juice in addition to comparatively small quantities of 'promine'. This 'retine' obtained from these mushrooms was identical in chemical components and physical characteristics to that obtained from animal tissues and urine, the latter being the major preparation source. It seems that a synthetic compound of 'retine' can be made available. (The paper referred to in this article is being presented by Dr. G. Foder of the University of Quebec jointly with Mr. Szent-Gyorgyi.)

Mushroom Growers' Association Bulletin No. 210
Since, and even before those first French growers discovered the art of controlled mushroom culture, beliefs existed that this ancient vegetable might be related to successful prevention of cancer. This

question was once again referred to in the M.G.A. Bulletin No. 210 published in June 1967. Afterwards a letter was received from a mushroom grower concerning this controversial question. This is what he wrote:

A very near relative who was seriously ill with cancer twelve months ago and was in fact given only a few weeks to live was persuaded by me to have about three pounds of mushrooms per week and is today remarkably well, much to the surprise of her doctor and to the specialist to whom she goes for a monthly check up.

On the strength of this the mother of a friend of mine who suffers from the same disease was also supplied regularly with mushrooms some six months ago and she too is responding remarkably well although four of her associates who went for special treatment with her ten months ago are now dead.

I am obviously not claiming anything regarding the mushroom, as the improvement in the cases mentioned could well be due to the treatment they are receiving from their doctors but to me the two cases cited seem to be a remarkable coincidence and I thought they might well interest other people.

From Meat to Mushrooms

The findings of American research chemist Dr. Arthur Karler, employed with a meat packing company, give a boost to the expansion of the cultivated mushroom. Dr. Karler considers that experts are today able to control the world's mighty mushroom crop in such a manner as to provide excellent protein for millions on the verge of starvation. In order to obtain such gigantic crops of mushrooms, Dr. Karler's experiments showed they could be grown on waste matter. He also maintained that the harvested mushroom protein would be as good as animal flesh. This project is now taking place with the object of selling more mushrooms to the American housewife and expanding cultivation to aid unfortunate people, many of whom do not know when their next meal will arrive.

Steak or Mushrooms

An interesting insight into the growing popularity of eating mushrooms as a sustaining meal is given in the March 1970 publication of American mushroom growers. In this issue of the magazine, *Brandywine Bugle*, a contrast is made with the present day appreciation of little mushrooms, when it is explained that the time may come 'when instead of plattering our steaks with mushrooms in sauce we will platter our mushrooms with bits of steak in sauce'. This is no doubt happening and will do on an increasing scale with the big upward trend in meat prices of the future.

The Booming Mushroom

The table opposite, obtained from The American Mushroom Institute, shows how production has almost doubled in the last ten years.

During 1968-69 almost three-quarters of the 189 million pounds grown in America were cultivated by mushroom growers in the Pennsylvania area. In the above table canned mushrooms are converted to trimmed fresh weight on the basis of 1 lb of canned dried weight to 1.538 lbs of fresh weight. Dried mushrooms are converted to fresh weight on the basis of 1 lb of dried weight to 10 lbs of fresh weight using the following formula: Dry lbs x 92.5 (moisture loss of dried product) divided by 9.6 (100 minus 90.4 moisture of original mushrooms) equals fresh weight.

MILLION POUNDS

Crop Year	Pennsylvania Production	U.S. Production	Imports Canned	Dried	Apparent Consumption
1959-60	—	108	2	7	117
1960-61	—	115	3	8	126
1961-62	—	127	10	9	146
1962-63	—	132	10	8	150
1963-64	—	131	14	8	153
1964-65	—	140	16	10	166
1965-66	93	156	21	7	184
1966-67	98	165	17	9	191
1967-68	113	181	34	10	225
1968-69	121	189	34	9	232

CHAPTER THREE

PROTEIN, VITAMIN AND MINERAL CONTENT

FOR A LONG time it was widely accepted and
endorsed by persons sadly misinformed that mushrooms contained little or nothing of real food value;
simply providing a luxury dish for those who could
afford them. With its appetizing flavour this fine
vegetable was mostly served to bring variety to other
dishes. This assumption has been entirely disproved
during the last thirty years and the mushroom, very
rightly, has come into its own as a valuable food crop.

It is now known that mushrooms contain a higher
percentage of protein than any other vegetable, with
the exception of green peas and the fabulous soya

bean. The mushroom is a tasty vegetable which can be served in an endless variety of ways, and, as with many meat dishes can provide a course for any meal. The crops are cheap to buy for there is no wastage, especially when we compare them with meat. A boon to the housewife, mushrooms are easy to prepare, need little cooking and are a real delicacy if simply served raw after washing. They provide a tasty food for everyone, and being easily digested are ideal for invalids. Providing the cultured mushrooms are clean there is certainly no need to peel them. Not only does the cultured mushroom bring one of the finest flavours to meals, it contains valuable health-giving ingredients, as we shall see.

Protein

Protein is one of the most essential bodily needs and meats contain the richest supply. Animal protein foods are generally quite expensive for the housewife. Vegetarians and other non-meat eaters for religious or health reasons must ensure that they receive an adequate daily supply of protein. Apart from peas, mushrooms contain the highest amount of protein of any European cultivated vegetable crop. Peas cannot be considered a vegetable to be served with every meal, but the mushroom will enhance any dish or can even be served as a main part of one.

From a study of *The Progress of Industrial Microbiology* by Worgan (Volume 8, 1968) it is revealed that the protein content of our cultivated mushroom is as high as thirty-six per cent dry weight but only three to four per cent fresh. So the dried mushroom is of excellent food value for it is a full protein food containing all the twenty-one amino acids necessary for good health. It was also shown that mushrooms have useful amounts of fat, are rich in B group vitamins and contain vitamins C and D. In addition it was revealed that mushrooms have a good supply of the minerals copper, iron and potassium.

From the *Handbook of Mushroom Culture* by A.M. Kligman, M.D., Ph.D., it will be seen that about sixty per cent of the total nitrogen in mushrooms consists of protein. On comparison with meat, mushroom protein was shown to have some thirty-five per cent of the biological value of casein. It was proved that human beings have remained in positive nitrogen balance by being fed mushrooms as the only source of protein. All the essential amino acids were identified as being present in mushrooms in varying degrees. Kligman also verified that niacin, the anti-pellagra vitamin, available in fresh mushrooms, fluctuates from five to ten times the amount in other vegetables such as carrots, lettuce, spinach and tomatoes. The niacin content of mushrooms was in fact shown to be almost equal to the amount found in pork or beef, which were always considered the richest sources. The daily bodily requirements of niacin necessary to enjoy good health is about 15-20 milligrams and there are some 6 milligrams per 100 grams of mushrooms.

High Protein Content of Crops

Studies of mushroom protein have been made at The Glasshouse Crops Research Institute, Rustington, Littlehampton, Sussex. Dr. Alfred Hayes, a microbiologist has proved that mushrooms could provide a good source of protein for helping to solve world starvation. He made a study of mushroom compost materials in terms of organic growth rates for different spore development systems.

In 1969 Dr. Hayes revealed some of his findings in an article entitled, 'Mushrooms, Microbes and Malnutrition' which appeared in *The New Scientist*. Dr. Hayes' findings were that the estimated yield potential from livestock (beef) farming would amount to about seventy pounds of dry protein per acre annually. At the same time he was able to reveal that many mushroom farms in England were yielding averages of 60-70,000 lbs of dry protein per acre per year. This means that mushroom farming could produce nearly 1,000 times the protein of livestock farming per acre. Of course it must be borne in mind that whereas the fresh mushroom contains only three to four per cent protein, the dried species has thirty-six per cent. So for the relief of world famine the dried mushroom could be classed as an exceptionally good source of protein. The soya bean contains the richest supply of protein of any crop in the world, being rated at over forty per cent. However, the mushroom stands supreme as a farm crop for producing the highest yield of protein per acre ever recorded. The soya bean as a farm crop can produce an average of six times the amount of protein as livestock per acre, but the mushroom far exceeds this.

World-Wide Interest

Other countries are also exploring the possibilities of the mushroom as a protein food. In particular this applies to America (see **From Meat to Mushrooms** in Chapter Two) and Japan.

Japanese researchers at Osaka Municipal University's Fukumoto laboratory have cultivated crops of mushrooms on beds made up of soya bean cake, rice bran and peat, laid on heat-sterilized straw. Mud mixed with 0.05 per cent of activated charcoal is then put over these materials. The charcoal provides good ventilation and the temperature is kept at 20°C.

Pernicious Anaemia

The protein content makes the mushroom a good food, but equally as important is the fact that it contains a rich supply of folic acid. Few foods are known to possess this valuable ingredient in appreciable quantities and some include spinach, brewer's yeast, kidneys and liver: the latter is one of the richest sources. Folic acid provides an essential bodily need for a healthy blood stream thereby helping to prevent such illnesses as pernicious anaemia. This disease is very prevalent, especially among women, even today. It was a Dr. Williams of Texas University in America, who, at the beginning of the Second World War, discovered that mushrooms contained larger amounts of folic acid than practically any other vegetable or meat, with the exception of liver. This fact caused a boom in the cultivation of the crop in America during the years that followed. They accepted the mushroom as a fine food cum medicine for treating this serious blood deficiency, which it is said to have done with success.

Food for Diabetics

The mushroom crop, containing no starch, serves a very useful purpose in providing sustaining food for diabetics in place of other vegetables such as carrots, onions, turnips and potatoes.

Vitamins

Both wild and cultivated mushrooms contain a good supply of vitamins. Cultured crops, from the findings of McCullum and Simmonds, proved to be a rich source of vitamin B_1 with several members of the B_2 complex. These findings confirmed the evidence provided by Kligman that 100 grammes of fresh mushrooms contain about 6 mg. of niacin; and as previously stated the daily bodily requirement of niacin is considered to be from 15-20 mg.

Over the years the work of many researchers including McCullum and Simmonds, Quakenbush, Peterson and Steenbock has shown mushrooms to have a good supply of thiamin (vitamin B_1) and riboflavin (vitamin B_2). C. Sumi also established that crops have a good amount of ergosterol, the source of vitamin D (the sunshine vitamin).

Vitamin C (ascorbic acid) present is equal to 3 mg. per 100 grammes of fresh mushrooms; the daily bodily need of this vitamin, which cannot be stored, is said to be some 30 mg. Citrus fruits, black currants, rose hips and in particular acerola cherries, contain the richest supplies of vitamin C.

A certain fluctuation tends to exist concerning expert findings into vitamin, mineral and other contents of mushrooms. This is considered to be mainly due to the growing medium: some manures and compost contain larger amounts of certain minerals than others. Also nutrition experts have sometimes obtained data from wild species and not the cultivated crop. As the wild mushroom is rarely sold in large quantities today we are mainly interested in the cultured species.

The variation in findings is illustrated from the copper content of mushrooms as shown by the following recorded analyses:

Bridges & Mattice, Food and Beverage Analyses, '1.79 mg. per 100 grammes'.

Anderson & Fellers. Proceedings of the American Society for Horticulture, 1942, vol. 41, p. 301, '.135 mg. per 100 grammes'.

Hodges & Paterson. Journal of the American Dietetic Association, 1931, vol. 7, p. 6, 'Mushrooms are a good source of copper, comparable

with liver, oysters, currants and chocolate'.
These findings clearly show that the copper content
depends on the growing medium and may vary
widely.

One outstanding feature about mushrooms is that
they will only grow in horse manure or organic
composts. This factor alone must greatly contribute
towards their goodness, taste, vitality and health-
giving properties.

As we have shown, mushroom crops contain a
good supply of vitamins and minerals plus folic acid,
the finest known ingredient for enriching the blood
stream and preventing deficiencies.

Mineral Salts
Mushrooms have a richer supply of ash content or
mineral residue than many meats and have double the
amount appearing in most vegetables. Refined foods
are sadly lacking in mineral and ash content, which
are important for health. Crops also contain calcium,
phosphorus, sodium, potassium, manganese, iron,
zinc: plus a fair amount of sulphur. Mushrooms also
have enzymes including trypsin, identical in every
respect to the enzyme of the pancreatic juices
produced in the stomach to aid digestion.

Whole Food
An indication of the food value of mushrooms is
revealed when it is made known that rats have existed
entirely on a diet of them for long periods. On
examination such rats have been found to enjoy an
equally good state of health as those feeding on a
mixed diet.

During the Second World War Hitler not only
decorated his U-boat commanders with 'iron crosses'
but ruled, on the advice of his experts, that all

mushroom crops should be set aside for submarine crews.

In more recent times the mushroom has been accepted as a food cum medicine for the prevention or cure of pernicious anaemia and it may possess far greater protective powers than is realized even today.

Compost Grown Crops

For years it was widely accepted that mushrooms, in common with such vegetables as marrows, pumpkins, radishes and cucumbers, contained little if anything of real food value. This assumption has long since been disproved for our mushrooms contain a rich supply of vital bodily needs in addition to a good amount of protein. This is understood when we consider that mushrooms and the other compost grown crops mentioned can only be successfully cultivated in a rich soil. For instance, members of the marrow family ·demand an entire compost heap to obtain full goodness of growth and nourishment. Being packed with vitality in the process of maturing they provide a store house of essential bodily needs. So mushrooms, thriving only in a rich compost, will not germinate in ordinary soil; this is perhaps why they make such appetizing dishes, full of goodness.

Low Calorie Food

The mushroom has the outstanding characteristic of being a very low calorie food. Fresh supplies contain only about 3 calories per 100 grammes, which equals about 32 calories to the pound. By comparison, old potatoes, raw, and peeled contain 70 calories per 100 grammes which equals 740 calories to the pound (approximately). So the mushroom as a food for supplying energy, is sadly lacking; but its low calorific value makes it one of the most suitable diets for 'weight watchers'. As progress has been made in civilization people tend to consider eating in relation to the pleasure it provides. This has resulted in an increasing percentage of people in western countries trying to solve the problem of obesity which affluent society often brings. Low calorie foods are sought in preference to those containing excessive starch; so mushrooms prove ideal for those on reducing diets.

Over twelve years ago it was established that mushrooms provide a vital nutritious food. Possessing an outstanding taste value they enhance other foods, bringing a fine flavour and zest to any meal. This helps to make the mushroom a popular dish, for no matter what may be good or bad for us, people generally, even when on a reducing diet, will still eat foods they like and which appeal to their taste.

A study of mushroom protein shows it to be similar to that of wheat and rye cereals. People on reducing diets can also get essential bodily needs from the vitamin and mineral content of mushrooms, which are both economical and easy to prepare. Long before the true value of this food was made known man always made a search for the mushroom, which was classed as an exotic dish. As a result mushrooms were for a long time considered an expensive luxury to be used sparingly for flavouring. This view persisted till it became possible to cultivate large crops under controlled conditions and market them at reasonable prices. It was not until the Ministry of Agriculture accepted the mushroom as a fine food crop that the way was paved for the extensive cultivation of recent years.

So the mushroom is a fine food ideal for retaining normal weight with a protein content high enough to somewhat resemble the flavour of meat dishes.

Advantages

Mushrooms are one of the few crops in which there is virtually no wastage but they do have to be sold and prepared soon after gathering. However, if not marketed fresh, crops may be canned, dehydrated, and, more recently — especially in America — frozen. All this presents tremendous possibilities for the mushroom crop as a food, providing of course that the vitality is not adversely affected by freezing.

An attraction about mushroom cultivation from the health point of view is that, owing to the essential need of crops to have an adequate supply of compost, they only respond to organic culture.

CHAPTER FOUR

MUSHROOM CULTIVATION

MUSHROOMS ARE FUNGI and in common with all such species grow and develop into vegetables without leaves, flowers, seeds and practically no stems. Our peculiar little mushroom matures without the aid of sunshine or even light; this being its most remarkable feature which allows the cultivation of crops almost anywhere. Over ninety per cent of mushroom growth occurs beneath the soil or seed-bed and it only appears above the surface at the last stage of growth. With no leaves mushrooms cannot carry out photosynthesis, so for this reason crops need large amounts of organic matter to feed on.

Wild Mushrooms

The exact manner in which mushrooms appear under natural conditions remains something of a mystery. They are closely connected with animals, horses, cattle and birds. Often wild species are eaten by eggs, fungi or bacteria. These little blocks harbouring so many unwanted seeds were often packages of unseen headaches and problems ahead for the unfortunate grower. Sterilized spawn is free from such setbacks, and, although it does not make mushroom growing child's play, many of the former hazards have now been eliminated.

Invariably failure to obtain a crop of mushrooms can be traced to errors in cultivation, incorrect times of planting and so on. All seeds have a very high percentage of germination as laid down by the Ministry of Agriculture regulations. It is therefore in the interest of seedsmen to ensure that their mushroom spawn will, if given the right conditions, germinate into good crops of mushrooms.

Sterilized mushroom spawn is prepared in laboratories from specially grown excellent crops of mushrooms of a good strain, from which master spores can be obtained. The spawn is inoculated, packed in special containers, and a steady temperature maintained during the process (70° F. till the spawn has taken). It is however advisable to obtain your spawn from a reputable firm of seedsmen with a wide market.

Seed-Beds

With no leaves and only short stalks, mushrooms need the compensation of vast amounts of organic matter in order to grow to maturity. So an abundance of decayed compost or animal manure is essential. Owing to the difficulties which may arise in obtaining horse manure a special mushroom compost is available for growing crops both commercially or in gardens. Such fertile compost appears under natural conditions, thus accounting for wild mushrooms.

Life starts with spores which are almost invisible

seeds like minute particles of dust, resembling the
spores of ferns but even smaller. As spores germinate
they produce mycelium which are grey-white strands
resembling threads from spiders' webs. Strands grow
very quickly into a thick living mass known as spawn.
The first tiny mushrooms appear as the spawn sends
up shoots in the form of tiny white pinheads to the
surface. These soon form the spherical shapes of the
tiny immature button mushrooms, which, if left to
develop may finally reach full maturity as large open
flat mushrooms. These little mushrooms are sup-
ported on short thick stalks with a membrane known
as a veil which soon disintegrates, revealing pinkish
coloured gills protecting the multitude of minute
spores within. As growth proceeds the mushroom is
called a cup, and, on reaching maturity, the top
becomes almost flat and the stalk increases in length.
Propagation under natural conditions is brought
about when the veil, on breaking, releases the spores
which fall out and are blown away in the breeze.
Some spores, a very small minority, settle, to produce
other crops.

pH Content

It is most important for mushroom growers to obtain
a correct pH value of the compost; this being closely
related to the amount of hydrogen present in the
moisture content. The pH grading, which can fluctu-
ate from 0 to 14, also accounts for the acidity or
alkalinity of the compost. Any pH rating below 7
means that it is too acid and readings over 7 show an
excess alkaline content. A chart is provided showing
values in colour ranging from purple for acid to deep
green for very alkaline, each change representing a
hydrogen value of ten. So if a compost shows a pH
value of five it is ten times more acid than if

recording a value of six. Neutrality is seven, which is the pH value of pure water. The correct pH value of a compost to make it ideal for mushroom growing should be between 7.5 and 8.5. Generally, fresh manure is far too alkaline for a good crop. Gypsum will not only dry out fresh manure but is really wonderful for neutralizing the alkalinity to facilitate quicker composting. Gypsum has in fact helped to remove the uncertainty from mushroom culture.

Places of Cultivation

There are a variety of places where this versatile little vegetable may be grown by the amateur gardener. More direct control can be exercised and there are greater chances of success if crops are grown under cover. Ideal places are sheds, cellars, garages, caves, tunnels, vaults, which can all be used for cultivation. In fact anywhere where there is an unused space provided it is dry, free from cold draughts, but ventilated. For inside culture boxes in tiers are ideal; this being the system adopted in mushroom houses on farms. More than ninety per cent of the U.K. mushroom production is by the tray system (separate boxes arranged in tiers). In some countries, Holland for instance, ninety per cent of production is from shelves.

The ideal atmosphere, temperature, and other essentials can be more readily produced under cover: whereas crops growing wild or cultivated in the open are limited to late summer and autumn months when natural conditions prevail.

Outdoor Culture

For success in growing crops in the open the grower needs lots of luck; the selection of suitable sites is also important. Beds are then made up and taken care of as for indoor cultivation. Frames may be used for such beds or they can be prepared in grassland or under trees, there being no hard and fast rules, for this vegetable has been known to grow in the most unlikely places. The beds need a 6-8 inch layer of compost and in many countries, especially America, some two weeks after the beds have been impregnated with spawn a 1 inch cover of fine topsoil known as 'casing' is applied. In England this casing layer is made up of a mixture of peat and chalk — the first country to introduce this method. About three weeks after this has been carried out (if the grower is fortunate), the first signs of the crop should appear like pinheads through the surface. Two weeks later, pests, diseases, animals, and weather conditions allowing, the first delicious mushrooms can be gathered. They will then continue to grow for many weeks from one impregnation of mushroom spawn. As with all compost-grown crops the goodness goes into the vegetables and for this very reason, after each successive crop has been cleared a complete new bed of compost must be introduced. The discarded beds make ideal rich compost for every type of garden vegetable or flowers and plants which do not demand so much goodness as the hungry mushroom.

With outdoor mushroom growing, luck and 'green fingers' go hand in hand for both amateur grower and the professional man with a lifetime of experience to draw upon. Both can succeed if sufficient interest is shown in attending to every detail. In spite of all the hazards and setbacks crops of mushrooms can be cultivated in the open. However, the mushroom crop presents a challenge to any gardener, and in order to make the prospects of success more certain, crops should whenever possible be cultivated under cover.

Today the compost used for growing mushroom crops in practically every country consists of substances like straw (wheat, barley and so on), hay, chopped corn, cobs (maize), brewer's grains, gypsum, ammonium nitrate, muriate of potash and similar substances. The ideal compost is of course horse manure, still available in some countries. A substitute based on a formula devised in England, with straw as the basic material, is used all over the world.

Preparation of Compost

For the amateur, mushroom compost is usually sold by the bag, which is sufficient to cultivate an area of up to 50 sq. ft. Additional requirements include up to two hundredweights of clean straw per bag of compost and 54 gallons of water. When only limited cultivation is taking place this amount is sufficient. On cultivations using up to ten bags of compost, straw chaff can be used. If the straw is long it should be chopped in smaller sizes for long straw is not suitable for making small heaps. (Brief details of cultivation are given in Chapter Five — **Mushroom Growing Kits**).

Miraculous Reproduction

It has been estimated that some sixteen billion minute spores are produced by a single mushroom. This amazing performance could constitute a record in the plant world. The reproductive power of the mushroom is nature's way of counteracting the many setbacks of climate, insects, pests and diseases which this strange plant has to survive to reach maturity and so allow the species to continue. If only one spore per mushroom survived it would be sufficient support for nature.

Defies Explanation

Nearly forty years ago Beverley Nichols, the well-known author, wrote a book entitled, *Down the Garden Path*. The book relates his experiences with mushroom growing which clearly indicate how unpredictable this crop can prove to be. Mr. Nichols planted a large amount of mushroom spawn in open fields in June. In spite of all the care and attention to detail not one solitary mushroom appeared. Yet the remarkable thing was that in a neighbour's adjoining field mushrooms appeared everywhere. This crop was simply growing wild, a free gift to the neighbour, who had not made the slightest attempt to cultivate it. Before Mr. Nichols had recovered from his surprise he noticed large flushes of mushrooms appearing on a vegetable marrow compost heap in his own garden. Enquiries about this showed that at the time the field was being planted with spawn his gardener crumbled up a brick of spawn and put it in the marrow bed just for luck. The luck prevailed for the gardener but not for Mr. Nichols, who had divided up hundreds of bricks of spawn into particles without getting a single mushroom, in spite of the fertility of the field. About a week later Mr. Nichols was surprised to find a cluster of mushrooms which had appeared in a corner of the garage. An explanation from the gardener solved this mystery when he made it known that this was the place where he deposited the bag which the bricks of mushroom spawn arrived in. No doubt the gardener was well versed in the art of growing mushrooms, for he told his master that you cannot keep them down.

Growers today do not have to contend with the problem experienced by Mr. Nichols so long ago. The advent of mushroom spawn has removed much of the uncertainty from the cultivation of this crop.

Sales

In England by 1971, fifty per cent of the crop was

Manures

In accordance with the indisputable evidence that horses are closely associated with wild species of mushrooms, the finest medium for culture has always been considered to be composted horse manure. Fortunately, we have excellent organic composts to replace horse manure for today's crops. Though it is debatable if such composts, for the amateur, have the cropping power of horse manure, there are undoubtedly advantages in the freedom from smells and so on. However, for those country people, few as they may be, who have manure available, the first problem of growing a crop has been solved. For the bulk of growers however, including farmers cultivating large scale commercial crops, other excellent organic mushroom composts can be obtained to replace horse manure. There are a number of established companies who specialize in supplying mushroom growing kits for the amateur. Some of the compost mediums have a background record lasting for over thirty years in aiding the mushroom grower, both amateur and professional, in solving the problem of the shortage of natural horse manure.

Preparation

Manure substitutes have one great advantage over horse manure in that they are completely clean, free from smells, insect eggs, weed seeds and so on. These points are most important and help make for greater success in growing, especially for the person completely lacking in experience. Having received the bag or bags of manure substitute it is simply mixed with straw and water added. Straw can be obtained from seedsmen, corn chandlers, or forage merchants. After such preparation the compost resembles leaf mould and is equally clean and pleasant to handle. These manure substitutes can be purchased in single bags for beginners trying their hand at garden crops or in tons for commercial growers. It has been amply proved over the years that such horse manure substitutes will pave the way for abundant crops of mushrooms, providing all the other necessary instructions are complied with and the grower really intends to get results.

As has been amply demonstrated in this book, mushrooms will not germinate in ordinary soils but only in the richest seed-beds, being unable to undergo the chemical changes for which daylight is vital. For this reason the supply of nitrogen and other essentials must be readily available in the composted beds. It has also been mentioned that after each crop has been cleared the spent beds make excellent all-round compost for practically every other garden crop. Most vegetables, except for vegetable marrows and cucumbers, are not so hungry feeders as the mushroom. So growers will have the advantage of a continuous supply of compost for the vegetable garden and flower beds.

Mushroom Growing Kits

In America, England and other countries, mushroom growing kits are available to meet the needs of the amateur gardener who simply wants to cultivate just another vegetable crop for the kitchen, or for part-time growers seeking profitable hobbies. With such kits explicit growing instructions down to the last detail are issued. For amateur growers who might be interested enough to master the skill of mushroom cultivation, some companies undertake to purchase all or part of the crops. This makes growing a worthwhile hobby with a fair competitive price given for any mushrooms surplus to requirements.

Compost

All things being equal, the backbone of a good crop of mushrooms lies in the compost, for as with all other organically grown vegetables the end product is closely related to the growing medium. So every gardener producing a really good crop of mushrooms, has, in effect, mastered the problem of making mushroom compost. When success has been achieved in making the right kind of compost much of the chance and element of doubt has been removed from mushroom cultivation.

Essential Requirements

Taking everything into consideration the mushroom is far from being an easy vegetable to grow, but it will bring greater interest to gardening and its successful cultivation is quite an achievement for the amateur gardener. No stage of the crop's growth can be left to chance, and for success throughout the growing period it is imperative to observe simple but necessary instructions, paying strict attention to detail and cleanliness. If these various safeguards are observed the cultivation of this delicious little vegetable can become a most fascinating and worthwhile hobby.

CHAPTER SIX

MUSHROOM RECIPES

WITH EVERY DISH, whether it be simply soup, sandwich snacks, salads, main meals or a banquet, the skill of the cook plays a most important part. Our probe into this unusual fungus, the mushroom, shows it to compare more than favourably with every other vegetable. For centuries mushrooms have brought a fine delicacy to cooking. Being sustaining, wholesome and delicious, the mushroom is one of the most versatile vegetables known to man. Because of its protein content and appearance the mushroom can be made to resemble meat dishes in a variety of ways. During the past twenty-five years, in the same ratio that meat prices have increased so the cost of mushrooms has been reduced. Although mushrooms contain far less protein than meat there is no wastage in the form of fat, bones, skin, gristle or shrinkage after roasting. For simplicity and speed in preparation the mushroom, as a food, is second to none, being easy to wash, slice, and cook in minutes. The cooking may be dispensed with entirely, for mushrooms are delicious if served raw after washing.

Important Note

When studying these recipes the reader is asked to remember that *flour* means stone ground flour with all its wheatgerm, bran and protein retained. *Salt* indicates biochemic or sea salt only. *Margarine* denotes brands made from vegetable oils. *Sugar* refers to the unrefined varieties, such as Barbados. *Rice* should be the brown, unpolished kind. All these ingredients are available at Health Food Stores.

Preparation

Mushrooms should first be washed, immediately before preparing a meal, by simply putting them in cold water for a few moments to remove soil or any other matter. They must not be rubbed unduly or left too long in water, and, to retain whiteness a small amount of lemon juice may be added to the water. It is important not to prepare mushrooms till just before cooking as they are apt to become dehydrated. Little or no other treatment is necessary, other than washing before cooking. It may be necessary in some cases to remove the tough part at the end of the stalks, which may need slight scraping. The white mushroom needs no peeling but the brown variety may require a very slight amount of peeling of the caps. Invariably, the less treatment given the better the results for the dish being served. Unlike the earlier wild crops the cultured mushroom is mostly very clean. A number of mushroom dishes follow, covering every aspect of the use of this fine vegetable. Some of the recipes received awards from The American Mushroom Institute.

Chilled Mushroom Soup

1½ pounds fresh mushrooms
⅔ cup chopped onions,
⅓ cup chopped celery, rib and leaves
⅓ cup thinly sliced carrot
1½ teaspoons whole back pepper
1 teaspoon salt
1 bay leaf
3 tablespoons olive oil
2 tablespoons flour
½ teaspoon ground thyme
2 tablespoons cold water
2 cups light cream or half-and-half

Rinse and dry mushrooms. Remove and slice stems. Place mushroom stems, onions, celery, carrot, black pepper, salt and bay leaf in a large saucepan. Bring to boiling point, reduce heat and simmer for ten minutes. Meanwhile, slice mushroom caps. Heat oil in a large skillet. Add sliced mushroom caps; sauté until golden. Blend flour and thyme with water; stir into sautéed mushrooms. Cook briefly, stirring often; remove from heat. Strain simmered vegetable mixture, discarding vegetables. Add sautéed mushrooms to liquid. Bring to boiling point; reduce heat, cover and simmer for ten minutes. Cool and chill thoroughly. Skim off as much surface fat as possible. Just before serving stir in cream. Garnish with snipped parsley, if desired. This soup is best served the day it is made. *Makes 6 to 8 portions.*

Mushroom Open Sandwich

4 slices of bread
2 ozs mushrooms
4 ozs finely grated cheese
seasoning to taste

1 oz margarine or cooking oil
  (vegetable)
1 lightly beaten egg
tomato, parsley

Toast bread lightly on one side only. Gently sauté the mushrooms in the margarine or vegetable oil and add the 4 ozs finely grated cheese, beaten egg and seasoning. Spread this mixture on the untoasted side of the bread, top each with a slice of tomato and place under a medium grill till cheese has melted. Garnish with sprigs of parsley.

Mushroom Toasted Rolls

½lb mushrooms
1 tablespoon margarine or
  vegetable oil

½ cup milk
1 tablespoon flour
salt and pepper

Wash and chop the mushrooms into small pieces and sauté in melted margarine or vegetable oil. Blend in flour and milk and stir till brought to the boil. Season to taste, toast the outside of the rolls and spread the mixture on the inside. Grill and serve hot.

Mermaid's Delight

1½ lbs white fish
1½ ozs flour
½ pint milk

5 ozs butter or vegetable oil
6 ozs Gruyère cheese
¾lb mushrooms

Put the fish into a pan with sufficient water, or fish stock to cover, season, cover and cook till the fish flakes easily. Melt 1½ oz of butter or oil in a pan and stir in the flour, add the milk, season and bring to the boil. Stir in the cheese and the flaked fish. Put this mixture into individual oven-proof dishes. Slice and sauté the mushrooms and heap these on top of each dish. Cover and bake in oven at 375 degrees F. (or mark 5) for ten minutes.

Mushroom and Yogurt Salad

4 ozs mushrooms
3 hard-boiled eggs
¼ cucumber
½ teaspoon grated
  horse-radish

¼ pint yogurt
2 large tomatoes
½ teaspoon dry mustard
lettuce

Finely chop mushrooms, eggs and cucumber. Blend the mustard and horse-radish with the yogurt, adding salt and pepper to taste. Stir in the chopped ingredients. Arrange lettuce leaves on a dish and spoon the mixture on top. Decorate with sliced tomatoes.

Gouda Salad

6 ozs diced mushrooms
2 hard-boiled eggs
1 minced red pepper
1 tablespoon chopped parsley

¼ pint plain yogurt
1 teaspoon dry mustard
6 ozs Gouda cheese
1 lettuce

Mix the mustard and pepper with the yogurt. Add the mushrooms, cheese and chopped whites of the hard-boiled eggs. Chill for one hour, turning the mixture with a spoon on two or three occasions. Line a bowl with lettuce leaves and pile the mixture into the centre. Chop the yolks of the eggs and mix with the parsley. Sprinkle over the surface of the salad.

Scandinavian Raw Mushroom Salad

¾ lb small button
  mushrooms
6 fluid ozs olive oil
freshly ground black pepper

1 crushed clove of garlic
1 teaspoon sugar
salt

Put all the ingredients, except the mushrooms, into a seal jar and thoroughly shake. Add the mushrooms. Seal and turn the jar gently. Marinate for 2-3 hours, turning the mushrooms in the dressing several times. Three ways of serving:

1. Just before serving add cucumber, skinned and

finely diced. Ideal for serving with fish.
2. Finely chopped raw celery may be used in place of cucumber if preferred.
3. Blend one tablespoon tomato ketchup with the dressing round the mushrooms and stir in 2 tablespoons chopped watercress and chicory. Serve with grilled steaks and cold meats. Also makes a good topping for hamburgers.

Mushroom Salad

Slice some washed mushrooms as thinly as possible and cover with French dressing (two-thirds oil to one-third vinegar, lemon juice or a mixture of the two), and chill for one hour. Sprinkle thickly with chopped parsley and chives, or a little grated onion or shallot.

Mushroom and Asparagus Salad

1 lb sliced fresh mushrooms
2 pimentoes (cut in strips)
2 tablespoons chopped chives
1 cup chopped celery, heart
and leaves
1 hard-boiled egg (sliced)
onion salad dressing mix
vinegar

Pour salad dressing over mushroom mixture and marinate for one hour. Arrange groups of asparagus tips and mushroom mixture on greens.

Gammon in Aspic

6 slices ham
2 tomatoes
1 pint aspic jelly
2 ozs button mushrooms
8 gherkins

Arrange slices of meat on serving dish. Pour over enough aspic jelly to partly cover. Arrange sliced button mushrooms, gherkins and tomatoes to decorate. Cover completely with remaining aspic and leave to set in a refrigerator.

Avocado Cream

2-4 ozs button mushrooms
2 avocado pears
2 spring onions
1 tablespoon finely diced

cucumber
1 tablespoon mayonnaise
paprika

Halve the pears and remove the stones. Scoop out the centre and sieve the fruit into a bowl. Blend with mayonnaise and season with salt and paprika. Finely chop onions and mushrooms. Mix these with the cucumber and turn in the avocado cream. Put the mixture into the pear cases and serve well chilled.

Soft-Boiled Egg on Spinach

½ lb mushrooms
2 lb fresh spinach
1 desertspoon finely grated
  onion

8 eggs
2 ozs butter
1 tablespoon finely chopped
  red pepper

Clean and cook the spinach using little or no water. Sufficient liquid will come from the spinach to cook it and allow some over. Put cooked spinach into hot serving dish. Slice the mushrooms and cook them in hot butter for about 4 minutes; season with salt. Cover the spinach with the sliced mushrooms. Put the eggs into boiling water and cook for 3½ minutes. Carefully remove the shells and arrange whole eggs on top of the dish. Scatter raw onion and red pepper over the whole dish before serving.

Cottage Cheese and Mushroom Savoury

1 lb cottage cheese
¾ lb mushrooms
2 eggs

2 oz butter
1 desertspoon grated onion
seasoning

Butter 4 individual ovenproof dishes. Reserve 4 mushrooms for garnish and chop the remainder. Heat the butter and lightly cook the garnish mushrooms. Put to one side. Simmer the mushrooms and onion for three minutes. Mix with the cheese and stir in the beaten eggs. Add plenty of seasoning. Pour into the dishes and bake in oven 350 degrees F. (or mark 4), for 45 minutes or until just set. Put the whole mushrooms in the centre of each dish 5 minutes before the end of the cooking.

Vegetarian Dishes with Mushrooms

We have proved the mushroom to be an ideal food for vegetarians, and now give a few selected dishes which are tasty and satisfying.

Mushroom Salad

½ lb small mushrooms	2 tablespoons vinegar
chopped herbs	salt and pepper
6 tablespoons olive oil	

Wash and thinly slice the mushrooms. Mix all the ingredients together in a salad bowl and marinate for one hour. Sprinkle with chopped chives and parsley just before serving.

Tomatoes with Mushroom Stuffing

¾ lb mushrooms
6 tomatoes
milk

Prepare the tomato cases. Cook the sliced mushrooms in a little milk, butter, margarine and seasoning. Drain and make up a white sauce using the liquid in which the mushrooms were cooked. Add the mushrooms to the sauce when it has thickened and boiled. Season. Fill into the cases and grill. Sprinkle with a little chopped parsley just before serving.

Nut Hamburgers

2 ozs cooked chopped	fried onions to flavour
mushrooms	1 egg
¼ lb rice	salt and pepper

¼ lb fresh breadcrumbs   pinch of mustard
¼ lb ground nuts

Boil the rice, mix all the ingredients together and shape into cutlets. Cover these with egg and breadcrumbs, then fry golden brown.

Vegetarian Roast

4 ozs mushrooms   1 onion
4 ozs wholemeal breadcrumbs   2 oz vegetable margarine
4 ozs grated cheese   1 teaspoon yeast extract
1 egg

Chop the onion finely and cook it with the chopped mushrooms in the fat for fifteen minutes. Add the grated cheese, breadcrumbs, egg and the yeast extract. Mix them all together and put in a greased baking tin. Bake in a moderate oven for 30 minutes until the roast is brown. Serve with parsley sauce, carrots, sprouts, potatoes baked in the skin and a garnish of watercress and sliced tomatoes.

Keeping Mushrooms

Mushrooms may appear from time to time in heavy flushes so growers have more than they need for their immediate use. Sometimes it is possible to buy mushrooms cheaply and in such cases they can be pickled or preserved. There are two methods of doing this; by pickling or drying the mushrooms.

Pickled Mushrooms

Depending on size and freshness, 1 lb of mushrooms will make from ¾-1 lb of pickled mushrooms.

Wash the mushrooms, which should be of the small or button variety. Cut the largest ones into quarters if they are more than 1 inch in diameter. Place the mushrooms in layers in a preserving jar, or pan. Between each layer put a liberal sprinkling of sea or biochemic salt. Stand the pan over a very low heat and periodically shake about until the mushrooms are tender. Put into jars together with some of the liquid which they will have made during the cooking and then fill the jars up with cold boiled vinegar. Add one peppercorn to each pound jar and seal. Leave standing for about two weeks before using. Delicious if served with salads.

Drying Mushrooms

This process of preserving is very simple and in their dried state mushrooms retain their protein, flavour and other vital goodness. The entire vegetable can be preserved or the stalks may first be removed and the tops preserved. First skin the mushrooms by removing the thin layer covering the tops of the caps. They can then be dried by placing them on trays in an airing cupboard. This can also be carried out by using a slightly warmed oven, where the mushrooms are left till becoming dehydrated, that is, when they are dry and shrivelled up. Mushrooms in this condition may be purchased from Health Food Shops but it is quite easy to dry them yourself. When perfectly dry they can be kept in bottles or tins till needed. Some people make holes in the caps of dried mushrooms and string them together to hang in a cool dry place. Dehydrated mushrooms must be hydrated before cooking.

Most of the recipes mentioned have been tried and tested by the British Mushroom Growers' Association.

We now introduce a few more specially selected recipes, famed in America, some of which were awarded prizes at contests sponsored by The American Mushroom Institute.

Sautéed Mushrooms

1 lb fresh mushrooms
½ teaspoon salt
$\frac{1}{8}$ teaspoon ground black

pepper
4 tablespoons butter or
margarine

Rinse, pat dry and slice the mushrooms, which will make about 5 cups. Heat butter or margarine in medium sized pan. Add mushrooms. Sauté over medium heat for 3-5 minutes or until tender. Sprinkle with salt and black pepper. Serve hot. *Makes 4-6 portions.*

Mushroom and Shrimp Delight

1¼ cups quick cooking rice
1 can (6-8 ozs) sliced
mushrooms
salt and ground black pepper
to taste
1 lb package frozen, peeled

1 jar (4¾ ozs) strained
apricots
1½ tablespoons butter or
margarine (melted)
and deveined shrimps
(cooked)
¼ cup sour cream

Prepare rice as directed on package; place in a 1½ quart buttered casserole. Add shrimps, mushrooms, apricots, sour cream, butter, salt and black pepper; toss gently. Cover and bake in a preheated moderate oven (350 degrees F.) for 20 to 25 minutes or until piping hot. *Makes 3-4 portions.*

Mushroom and Peppers Italian

1 lb fresh mushrooms
2 large green peppers
1 medium onion sliced
¼ cup olive oil
2 large tomatoes, peeled and
sliced

¾ teaspoon salt
$\frac{1}{8}$ teaspoon ground black
pepper
$\frac{1}{8}$ teaspoon oregano leaves
$\frac{1}{8}$ teaspoon basil leaves
teaspoon garlic powder

Rinse, pat dry and slice mushrooms (makes about 4 cups). Slice green peppers into ½ inch strips. In a large skillet heat oil. Add mushrooms, peppers and onion; sauté until mushrooms are golden. Add tomatoes and seasoning; stir gently. Cover and simmer 20 minutes, stirring occasionally. Serve with meat or eggs. *Makes 6-8 portions.*